WHERE'S SANTA'S SUIT?

MARTIN CHATTERTON

Little Hare Books
an imprint of
Hardie Grant Egmont
Ground Floor, Building 1, 658 Church Street
Richmond, Victoria 3121, Australia

www.littleharebooks.com

Illustrations copyright © Martin Chatterton 2012

First published 2012
This edition published 2013

Cataloguing-in-Publication details are available from the National Library of Australia

ISBN 978 1 742977 06 5

Designed by Martin Chatterton
Additional design by Xou Creative (www.xou.com.au)

Printed through Phoenix Offset
Printed in Shen Zhen, Guangdong Province, China

5 4 3 2 1

WHERE'S SANTA'S SUIT?

MARTIN CHATTERTON

LITTLE 🐇 HARE
www.littleharebooks.com

It's the night before Christmas at the North Pole ...

The presents are wrapped, the decorations are in place and all over the world, excited boys and girls are tucked up safely in bed.

There's just one problem.

Santa can't find his clothes!

And if Santa can't find his clothes, then Christmas will have to be cancelled!

We need to get Santa dressed
before the clock strikes twelve!
Can you find Santa's clothes
before it's too late?

There's another problem.
Santa's pet polar bears have
escaped. Can you round them up?
There are eight in every room.

Santa also needs his lucky charms.
He won't leave home without them.
There are three in every room!

The Basement

The first thing Santa needs is his socks. Mrs Santa says they are somewhere in the basement, but you'll have to look hard to spot them. They're red with white spots.

Santa's charms are a fish on a dish, a soap on a rope, and a dog on a log.

Good hunting! Remember the bears ...

One of Santa's helpers is slightly different. Can you spot him?

The Kitchen

Now we need Santa's undies. Santa thinks he left them in the kitchen. I hope you find them before Cook mixes them into the Christmas pud!

Don't forget Santa's lucky charms. There's a space-cat, a hat-cat, and a fat cat (with a bat). And the eight bears.

There's one more puzzle in the kitchen ...

One of the elves turned a banana bright blue. Can you find it?

The Workshop

This is the room where the presents are made. And somewhere here is Santa's singlet. Once we find it, he won't look quite so rude!

Did you remember the charms? Hidden in the workshop are an electric eel, a performing seal, and an old ship's wheel.

And those bears ...

There's one more puzzle. The elves have made one submarine different. Can you find it?

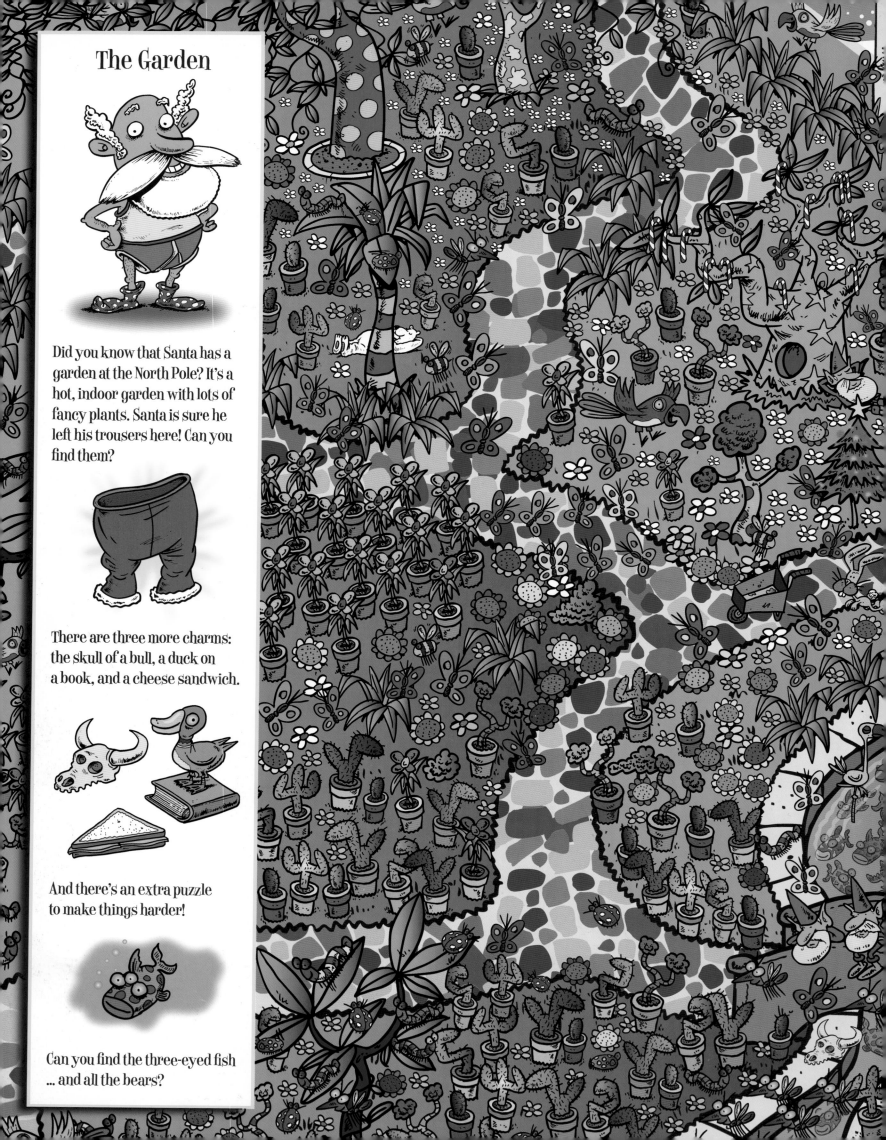

The Garden

Did you know that Santa has a garden at the North Pole? It's a hot, indoor garden with lots of fancy plants. Santa is sure he left his trousers here! Can you find them?

There are three more charms: the skull of a bull, a duck on a book, and a cheese sandwich.

And there's an extra puzzle to make things harder!

Can you find the three-eyed fish ... and all the bears?

The Paint Shop

This is where the presents are painted. Sometimes the elves paint things the wrong colour! Like Santa's best boots. See if you can spot them before someone paints them pink!

Santa still needs his three charms. Can you find an old-fashioned phone, a dinosaur bone, and a green saxophone? Good luck spotting those bears!

There's one more puzzle. A penguin has sneaked in. Can you find him?

The Swimming Pool

Santa left his spotty shirt here last time he had a swim. See if you can find it.

Santa's charms aren't easy to find. There's a brown crown, a lime-green bean, and an old blue shoe.

The bears love the pool. Can you find all eight?

There's one last puzzle. One of the Nessies is different. Can you spot which one?

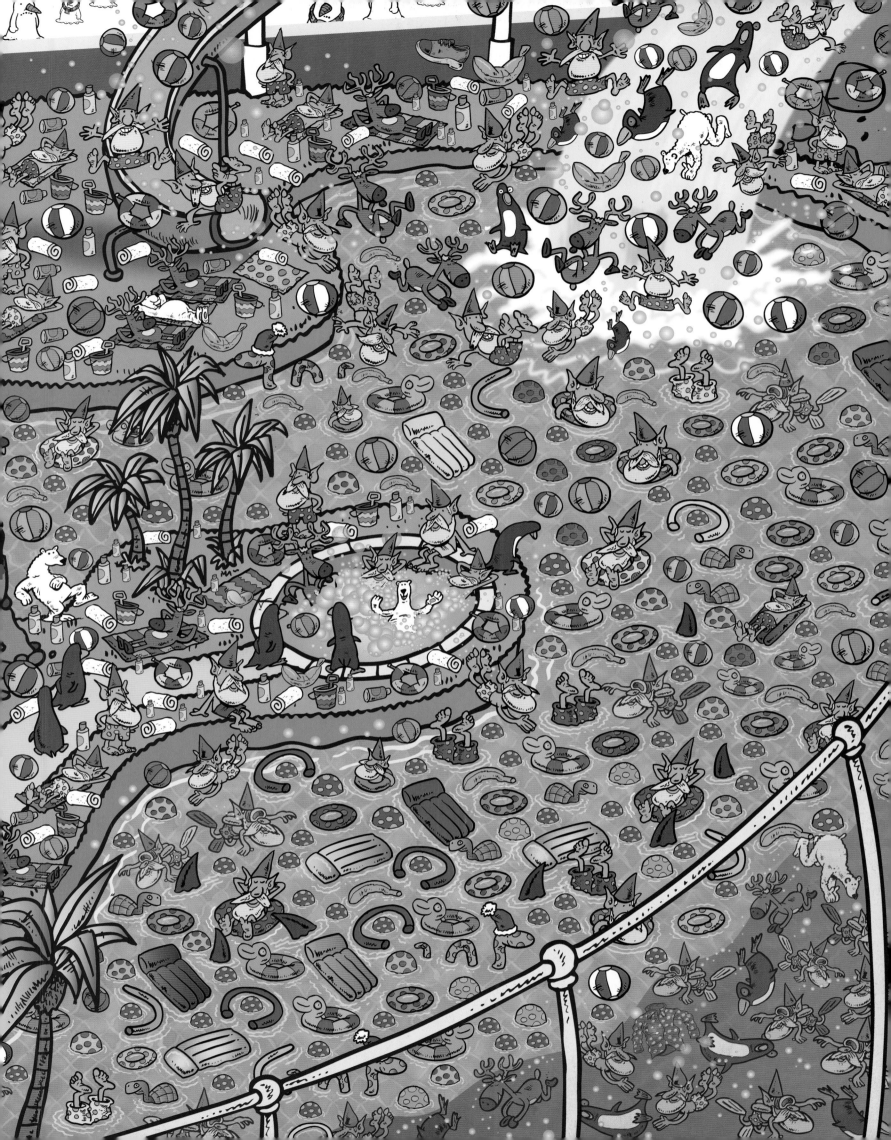

The Packing Room

Hidden in the packing room is Santa's waistcoat. I hope it hasn't been packed up as a present!

There are three more charms: a fox in a box, a box on a fox, and a box of foxes.

And don't forget the bears!

Can you spot which of Santa's helpers is the odd one out?

The Dining Room

Santa is starting to look more like Santa, but his jacket is somewhere here.

You still need to find those lucky charms! There is a Martian on a mission, a giraffe who likes fishing, and a shark who's been kissing. And the bears ...

One of the penguins has eaten too much and turned a funny colour! Can you spot him?

The Dormitory

It's night-time but not all the elves are in bed! Somewhere here is Santa's big belt. Can you spot it?

Santa's charms are here, too. There's a lizard, a wizard, and a lizard wizard!

The bears are sound asleep!

The elves have left socks and undies everywhere! But only one pair of undies is spotty! Can you find them?

The Playground

Now Santa is dressed. There are just a few things left to find. He thinks he dropped his gloves.

There are three more charms: a frog on a hopper, a dog with a chopper, and a hog-shaped bottle-stopper!

The bears are here, too.

There's only one all-white penguin in the playground. Can you find it?

The Roof

The elves are getting the presents ready to go on the sleigh. Santa just needs his hat before he blasts off.

We have nearly all Santa's lucky charms. There are three more here: a rock, a lock and a clock. The bears are hiding – look closely!

Can you find your way through the maze of boxes from the attic hatchway to the furthest chimney?

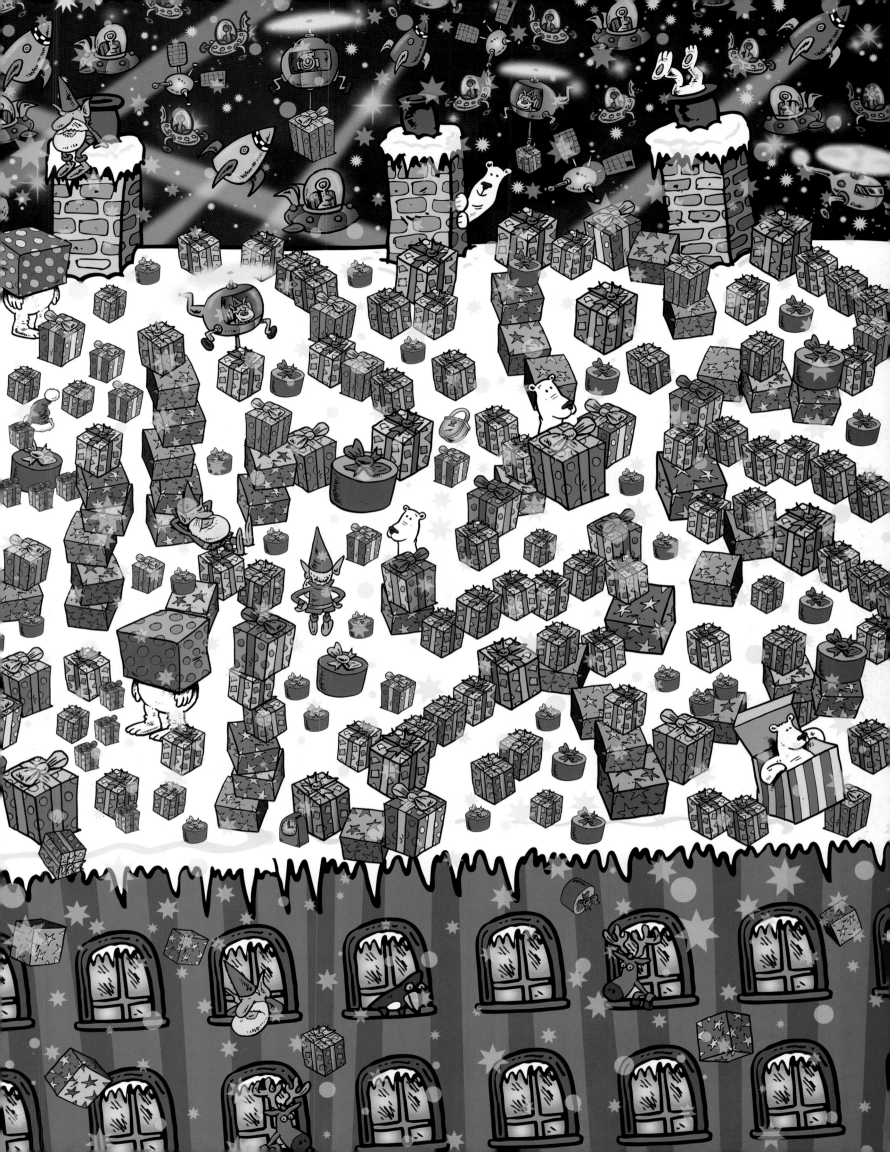

Blast Off!

You've saved Christmas! Well, almost ... there's one more thing Santa needs before he can start delivering presents – his moon glasses.

The countdown has begun. Ten ... nine ... eight ... seven ...

Don't forget those last three lucky charms: there's a parrot, a carrot and a parrot on a carrot. Six ... five ... four ...

And find those bears!

Three ... two ... one ...

CHRISTMAS!

The Kitchen

The Garden

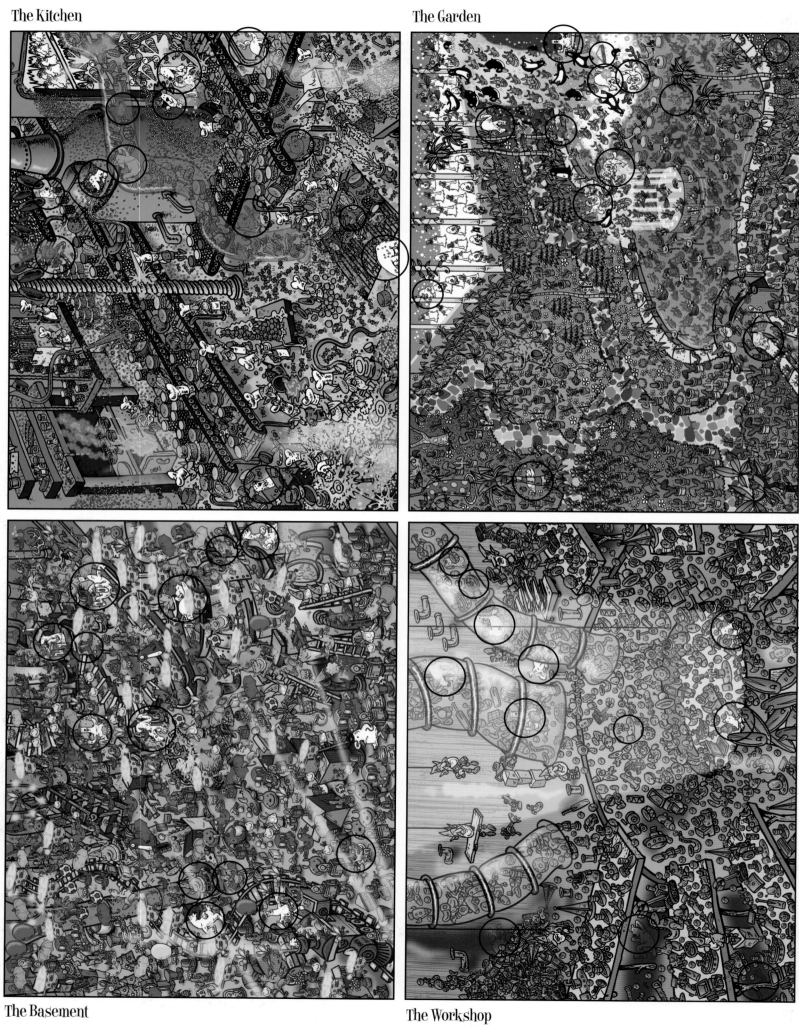

The Basement

The Workshop

The Swimming Pool

The Dining Room

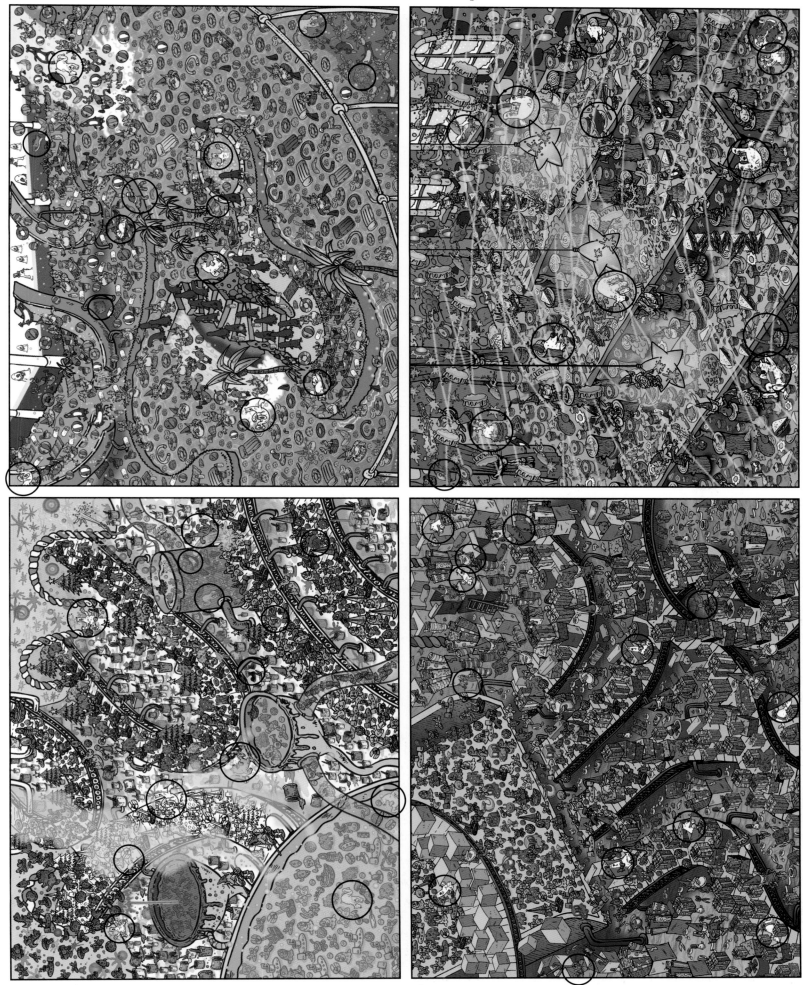

The Paint Shop

The Packing Room

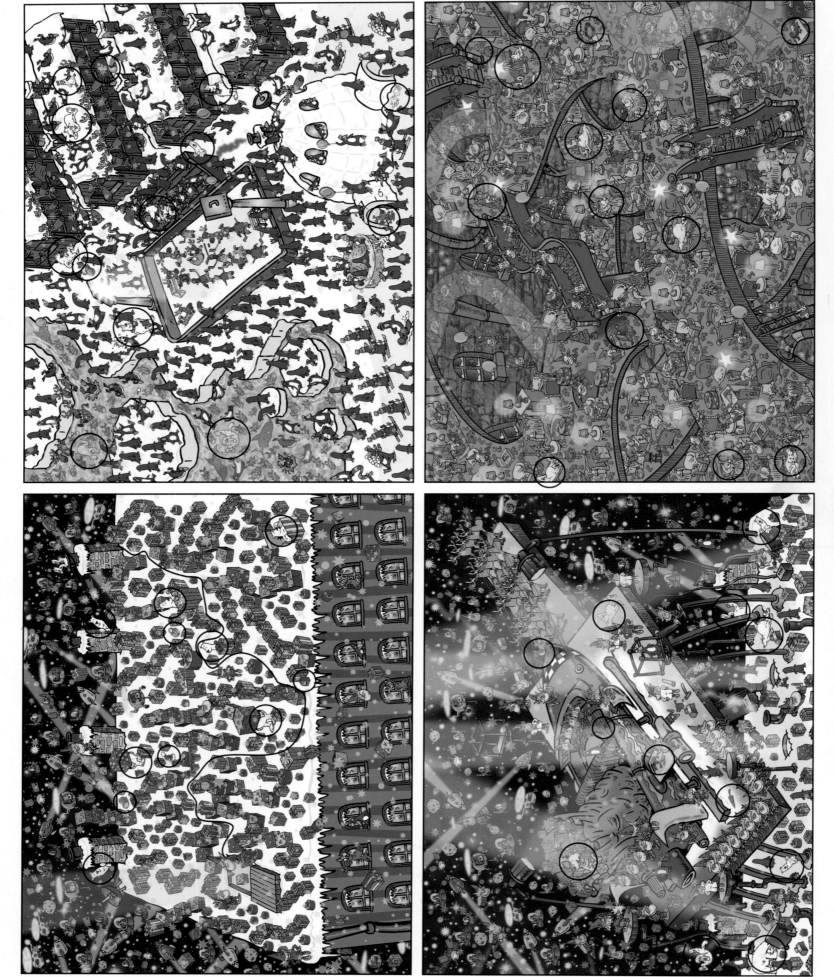

The Playground

The Dormitory

The Roof

Blast Off!